Retailing in Action

Retailing in Action

Salon Professionals!

Conquer the Obstacles of Selling Retail Forever

Jeanne Degen

Rev. date: 12/30/2022

To order additional copies of this book, contact:
Xlibris
844-714-8691
www.Xlibris.com
Orders@Xlibris.com
849843

DEDICATION

I would like to dedicate this book to William Decker who has been
a great friend and mentor throughout my many years in the beauty
industry. I will always be thankful for his time, wisdom and friendship.

CONTENTS

ACKNOWLEDGEMENTS

I would like to acknowledge Mimi McCarthy for all her contributions in writing this workbook, Emmy Intoppa for all the research and efforts put into creating this book, and Richard W. Huntley Jr. for the endless hours put into editing this book to make it a success.

CHAPTER ONE

COMPASSIONATE RETAILING

What thoughts come to your mind when you hear the word retailing? Jot them down before going forward.

_____

_____

Are your thoughts about retailing positive or negative? Why?

_____

_____

Many stylists reject retailing because they see it as "selling" in- stead of another means of helping their clients. These salon professionals don't realize that selling retail products should come as naturally to them as selling clients a style, color, or cut – which they do every day!

- ❏ In this chapter I will go over the importance of re- tailing for salon professionals and explain why it is such a crucial component of building a strong client base.
- ❏ I will give step-by-step instructions outlining how to conduct a successful consultation in order to get clients to talk about issues they are having with their hair. I will then show you how to give your clients solutions to all of their hair concerns.
- ❏ I will also explain the importance of upselling services to your clients, making them aware of all the options they have to change their hair if they desire.

So let's get started!

Professionals who think that they are not sales people are mistaken. They sell their skills, their talents, and their knowledge every day, in every way.

Keep in mind that we stylists must give our clients reasons why they NEED certain products. Therefore, you have to know what you are selling. You must be educated on the product. You should use it your- self. It is important to have first- hand knowledge of how the product works so that you know its benefits. It's hard to sell something you don't understand. Here are 10 step- by-step points to help you conquer the difficulties with retailing that so many salons experience.

1. After a client has been greeted and is seated in your chair, the consultation should begin.
2. You should request the client's per- mission to ask a few questions about her hair before you get started.
3. At this point, you can begin to ask probing questions that would make it easy for the client to tell the history of her hair. Ask the client what she has done in the past that she liked and what she did not like. Ask the client what she likes about her current hairstyle and what she is happy with and does not want changed.

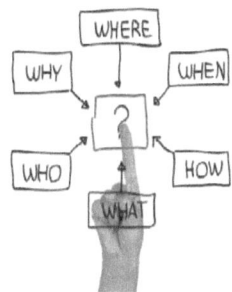

It is extremely important to allow the client to tell you what issues and problems she is having with her hair. What you are doing is getting the CLIENT to tell you what is wrong with her hair instead of insulting her by YOU telling her what is wrong with her hair. This tactic is much more diplomatic, and she will respect you much more with this approach. Essentially, you are asking permission from the client for you to discover information about her hair from her, so she, in turn, will be more apt to listen to your response, expertise and knowledge.

What questions will you ask to help your client feel comfortable sharing with you? How will you help your client open up?

_____

_____

_____

_____

_____

4. At this point, you will want to ask the client, "If there was anything you could change about your hair what would that be?" Often times, clients don't realize all the options that we, as hairstylists, have to offer. I make this part of the questioning a fun game, and I may pretend to be a genie, who can grant the client 5 wishes, without limitations, to change her hair.

"More volume," "shinier hair," "straight and less frizzy," "healthy looking hair," "more texture in my hair," are just a few of the many things a client might suggest about her hair to you.

What other ways could you help your client think of changes?

_____

_____

_____

5. Now you should repeat back what the client has told you to verify you heard everything correctly.
6. After the client agrees that you heard correctly, here is your chance to offer options that will help fix the problems the client has just listed.

This is an opportunity for you to explain the different services offered at the salon and all the different options available to the client to help her with her hair concerns.

For example, I had a variety of menus in my salon reception area that explained the different services we offered. Many times clients were not even aware of

these services. If the client mentioned to me that she was having hair volume issues, I would bring her our texture menu to show and explain all the different options we offered for volumizing and style support without having to go curly.

If the client complained about dull, frizzy hair, I would go over our menu choices for re- texturizing hair and explain all the options and services we offered to take care of the problem. At the end of this workbook, I have included examples of the texture menus I offered in my salons, so feel free to look them over for ideas.

Be sure not to overwhelm the client with too many things at once. The idea is to educate her about the different solutions you can offer her and plant a seed for her next visit.

7. Once you have finished with this portion of the consultation, you then want to ask the client what products she is currently using. If the client answers with a drug store brand, don't gasp, just gently tell the client that you will be using "such-and-such" products today, and that they will help with the hair concerns the client has explained. Remember stylists: you are not selling a product, you are selling a solution!

How is selling a solution better than selling a product?

_____

_____

8.   Next, when the client moves to the shampoo bowl, you should remind her of the issue with her hair that was dis- cussed during the consultation. For example, let's say the client mentioned that her hair lacked volume, then you would want to  briefly say, "I will be using our volumizing shampoo and conditioner." Then give her the best scalp massage ever. She will be greatly appreciative.

9.   When the client gets back to the chair, you will then begin the service. When you are applying product, you should be sure that it  coincides with the issue the client shared about her hair. For example you should say, "I will be using this shine product that will help to de-frizz your hair and give you great shine."

During the service, you should take the time to educate your client on how to use each product and let her hold the products as you are using them. This enables the client to feel ownership of the products she is holding.

10.   And finally, after the service is complete, you should go to the shelves and pick out the products you used on your client and set them up in front of the client. This is the time to review the products with the client. If the client suggests she cannot purchase them all, for whatever reason, you should recommend the most important ones to get her started.

Remember stylists, your client is a walking billboard for you. You want to make sure she knows how to obtain the style as well as you do. This is especially true if the style is new to her.

You need to keep in mind, if you, the stylist, don't know the problem, how can you give a solution? All this points to the importance of stylists knowing the science of hair and knowing products and their ingredients so they can prescribe the right antidote.

A stylist needs to realize the important role that professional products play in addressing hair problems and how much more effective they are than drug store brands. Chemically treated hair can often times be dry and fragile, especially if the client isn't taking precautions by replacing the nutrients that  the chemicals remove. This is called controlled damage. When you chemically treat hair, its natural proteins are depleted and need to be replaced by the right product. For example, if you go to the bank and constantly withdraw money without making any deposits, you will be in the negative. The same is true with hair. If you are depleting without replacing, the hair will eventually not be able to tolerate any chemical services until the hair is repaired. Most clients automatically believe that when their hair feels dry and brittle, they need moisture. Most often that is exactly what they don't need. Adding moisture may only add to the problem.

Protein is what will help to rebuild the hair back into a healthy state. I can't tell you how many salon professionals do not know this.

I studied Trico analysis (the study of hair) for years and be- came very knowledgeable about what hair needs and what to look for when determining the right product for people to use. Porosity and elasticity of the hair are two crucial parts to take into consideration when determining the damage of the hair and what can be done to restore it to health.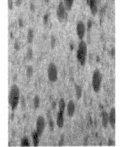

Scenario 1: Ellen's hair is breaking and feels like a scouring pad. Every time she combs or brushes her hair, pieces of hair snap and break off. Her hair feels hard and rough even when it is wet. She has been getting protein treatments because her stylist told her the protein is sup- posed to stop breakage and will help to rebuild the hair. She is using a professional fortifying protein shampoo and conditioner at home. But so far, nothing is working and her problem is getting worse.

Scenario 2: Nancy's hair also has a lot of breakage. Her hair feels dry, brittle, looks dull, and is very weak. When her hair is combed when it is wet, it stretches like a rubber band and then breaks. Her hair lacks shine and body and appears limp with no life at all. She is getting moisturizing treatments from her stylist. Since her breakage began, she has started getting these treatments weekly and follows it up with a professional hydrating shampoo and conditioner, but her problem has gotten worse.

I can't tell you how many times over the years I have seen stylists recommending the wrong products, a.k.a. the wrong solution, resulting in a client's hair

not being treated properly. Most of the time, the client will blame the product. This is why it is so important the stylist knows what to prescribe.

In scenario 1, the problem is that Ellen's hair needs a higher concentrate of hydrating treatments and products. Ellen should be using a professional hydrating shampoo and conditioner to help solve her problem.

In scenario 2, Nancy's hair needs a higher concentration of protein in her home maintenance products. In addition, she would benefit from in-salon deep protein treatments.

So how does the stylist manually tell the difference? Wet the hair, take a strand of hair between your two fore fingers and wrap the hair around each finger. Now pull. If the hair stretches like a rubber band and then breaks, this is a good indicator that the hair needs protein. If the hair does not have any pull and return or flexibility and feels hard and rough when it is wet, this is a good indicator that the hair needs moisturizing treatments.

To test for porosity of the hair, take a wet strand of hair be- tween your thumb and fore finger and slide up the hair shaft towards the root of the hair. If the hair has a rough feel to it, this means the cuticle is open and the hair is very porous. If your fingers glide more smoothly along the hair shaft, this means the cuticle is more intact. If the hair is more porous, it is a good indicator that the hair most likely may need protein.

If the hair is very elastic and is mushy when wet this is a good indicator that the hair will need more protein. If the hair is dry and feels hard and rough when wet this is a good indicator that the hair needs more moisture.

What I have been describing here are just a few additional tests you can use when you are trying to determine the overall condition of your client's hair.

Protein and moisture work together synergistically to produce a healthy head of hair, and neither can work well without the other. Keeping the hair balanced between these two entities is very important. Achieving the proper balance involves using the right combinations of protein and moisture based on what the hair needs.

When clients shop in a drugstore, they will not have the professional opinion

that a hairstylist can provide about what their hair is lacking and what it needs. They often just grab a product advertising what they THINK their hair needs without actually KNOWING what their hair needs. This information can only come from a salon professional.

Professional products contain different forms of protein that are broken down and absorbed by the hair. Drug store brands don't always contain the same types of protein as professional products. Professional products also contain the right balance of vitamins and moisturizing elements which are important for healthy hair. Drug store brands may not always contain the same ingredients in the same composition; therefore, they may be cheaper but are not always beneficial to the hair.

You can use your expertise to educate your clients about the superior ingredients in your products over those found in drug stores. Then they will understand why your products are a little more expensive. They may cost more to buy, but they produce the desired results. Your clients can stop searching for a bar- gain priced solution that doesn't exist.

Choosing products to use and sell in your salon is very important and needs to be supported by your salon team. You must choose products and companies in which you believe. So ask yourselves, "Do we believe in these products and love the results they produce?"

"Do we love the look, feel and smell of the products?" Remember clients of- ten buy on scent alone. You also need to

ask yourselves, "Do the products we sell give fabulous results the very first time we use them on clients?" It is important that you choose products that you truly believe are the best for your clients be- cause they should also be the products you use yourself.

What products can you confidently recommend to your clients right now?

_____

_____

_____

_____

_____

What products should you consider adding to those in your salon?

_____

_____

_____

_____

_____

 Successful retailing in the salon will elevate you from a mediocre stylist to a dynamic one. Your customers will appreciate your knowledge. They will appreciate you for taking the time to show them how to duplicate their styles at home with the right professional products.

As a stylist, imagine how difficult it would be for you to not use any products; imagine just using water to try to create a perfect style in your hair.

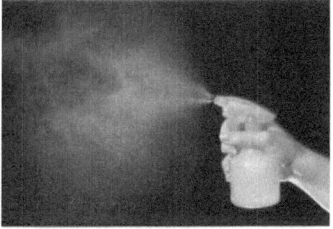

Remember..............

Know all you can about the products you are prescribing.

 Use the products yourself and familiarize yourself with all their benefits and how they work for you.

Always establish a need by listening and asking questions throughout your client's service.

Describe to your clients the products' features and how they will benefit their hair. Be sure you address any hair issues your client has told you about.

Demonstrate the use of the product on your clients. Educate them on how to do it at home.

Involve your customers with the product. Let them hold it, smell it, and feel its consistency. Show them the amount of the product they will be using. Over doing will end up with bad results, and clients will blame the product saying it makes their hair greasy, flat, etc.

Make the decision that you will suggest and recommend products to each and every one of your clients, old and new. Keep this in mind: **If you don't ask your clients to purchase products, someone else will.**

Remember, talking to clients about their hair is a priority. Do not start off their visits by asking them about their love life or their social status. Talk about hair.

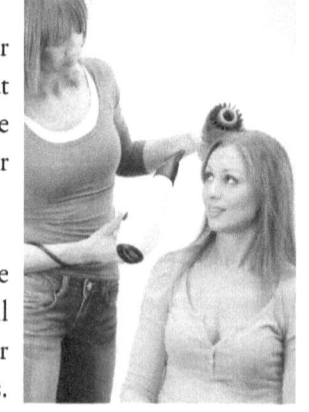

If you talk about, demonstrate, and educate your clients on their hair and the different products that will benefit them, they will love it. There will be plenty of time to chat about the other things later when they come back again and again.

Retailing is all about helping clients. It can make them feel better about the look they created. It will make them feel more confident. It will fix their hair dilemma, and they will think you are a genius.

When you look at retailing as helping someone find a solution, do you still feel like a salesperson? You are selling them prod- uct, yes, but only because it solves their problem. You only have the very best intentions.

Now we need to talk about retail goal set- ting. One way to set retailing goals for yourself is to start by setting a goal to sell one or two products per day. You can gradually increase that number. It is amazing how quickly you can reach a goal of selling just one or two products to 50% of your clients daily.

What retailing goals will you set?

_____

_____

_____

_____

When your retail sales are down, analyze what you are talking about with your clients. Change your approach a bit and stay focused on hair. It is amazing how easily this works. It is truly effortless when you actually care about your clients.

Selling retail in the hair industry is not "selling" if you are "helping." It is up to you to choose how helpful and considerate you want to be. In a world where so many people feel desperate to be heard and cared for, this compassionate retailing is a sure way to experience success.

CHAPTER TWO

OVERCOMING RETAILING AND UP-SELLING OBSTACLES

Would you like to know how to involve your stylists in retailing? Would you like to discover how elite resources in the industry overcome up-selling obstacles? Would you like to learn productive ways to assist your staff in retailing successfully?

In this chapter, I will include the tips and strategies that I have taught in my classes, and used in my own salons, that have proven to be the most successful. In addition, I will cover promotions and incentive programs for successful retailing.

So let's get started!

Here are some of the excuses I have heard from stylists about why they do not sell products, along with my responses to them.

1. **I am not a sales person.**
   However, every time you, the stylist, suggest a style change or recom- mend a color service, you are selling your own taste, skills, and knowledge.

2. **I don't want to sound pushy.** So don't push! Your clients come to you specifically for your advice and expertise. When they leave your chair they are looking their very best. It is important that you educate your clients on how to style their own hair and that you prescribe the right tools and products for clients to use at home; products that you have chosen specifically for their hair.

3. **The products are on display; if clients want some- thing, they will buy it.**
   As much as our staff would like to believe this statement, clients need a stylist's professional advice and guidance. An attractive display is important. It grabs a client's attention, but it doesn't provide clients with the knowledge of which products are best suited for their hair. Products do not sell themselves.

4. **I'm afraid of selling.**
   I have always been a firm believer that the antidote to fear is knowledge. The more comfortable and knowledgeable you are, the more confident you will be in selling.

5. **They won't buy no matter what I do.** I can't tell you how many times I have heard stylists say this. Then when I watch them with a client they talk about everything other than product.

Then at the end of the service, the stylist will say, "Are you all set with products?" If stylists are not explaining the products that they are using, and they don't establish a need with a client for the client to be using particular products, then they will NOT get the client to buy. I always told my staff, "You are selling a solution, not a product."

Successful retailing doesn't just happen. It is important for salon owners to learn how to prepare their stylists to sell.

What excuses have you heard? How have you responded to them?

_____

_____

_____

_____

When owners set out to discuss retail with their stylists, they need to be aware that it is much more involved than just having a stylist sell product. There are many things an owner can do to help a stylist feel more excited and secure when selling a product.

 First and foremost, a salon must carry products that will motivate and excite both staff and clients.

Once you have chosen products, be sure you provide adequate training for your staff. I cannot emphasize this strongly enough. Knowledge of a product brings confidence and is crucial in order for a stylist to feel comfortable selling. Many manufacturers offer product knowledge education classes as a complimentary service.

If the stylist is aware of all the benefits and features of a product, she will be more apt to sell. It is also important that the stylist uses the products in her own hair. I used to send my stylists home with different products to use themselves each week so they could become acquainted with all the products we stocked.

To be successful with retailing, it is essential to invite everyone on your team to be part of the process. As always, it starts with education. Remember, you should work with a company that will provide staff members with the training they need to understand their products inside and out. Talk with your staff about what products they like and what products they don't like. It's a team effort.

One incentive for selling that I used, in conjunction with my product companies, was to hold stylist sales competitions.

These always bring out the competitive spirit in everyone; so create weekly and monthly sales contests to motivate your stylists to sell.

I would ask my sales consultant, from each distributorship I used, to provide some fabulous prizes for the contest winners; prizes that would bring excitement to the staff such as blow dryers or thermal irons. Other examples of prizes I would offer were a "Night on the Town" or gift certificates to a particular store or restaurant.

Another retail incentive program that was extremely popular with my staff was one I called "Celebrate the Small Stuff."

This program actually tripled my retail sales in less than three months. I am a strong believer in using positive reinforcements to motivate my staff, rather than negative consequences. So let me share with you my "secret formula."

1. **Provide Constant and Consistent Focus.**

   ❑ I would have my entire staff meet once a month to re- view their goals and to celebrate all the successes of my staff.
   ❑ I would meet with, or call, the salon manager three times a week to discuss goals and to review which staff members were achieving them and which of the staff needed more coaching.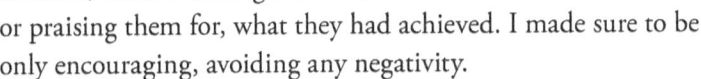
   ❑ I would meet with, or make weekly phone calls to, each staff member, either coaching them on, or praising them for, what they had achieved. I made sure to be only encouraging, avoiding any negativity.

2. **Have Robust Stylist Incentive Plans.**

I put together stylist incentive plans that provided stylists with the opportunity to make bonuses of up to 25% of their monthly retail sales. For example:

   • When any of my stylists sold up to $100 of product in a month, they received a 10% commission check.
   • When stylists sold between $100-$200 of product in a month, they received a 15% commission check.
   • When stylists sold over $200 and up to $1,200 of product in a month, they would receive a 20% commission check.
   • When stylists sold over $1,200 of product in a month, they would receive a 25% commission check.

3. **Have a Manager's Incentive Plan (based on monthly goals).**

   • The manager would receive $200 if 50% of the stylists met their retail goals.
   • The manager would receive $300 if 100% of the stylists met their retail sales goals.
   • The manager would receive an additional $200 if the salon had a 20% increase for the same month from the prior year in chemical sales.

I always made a very big deal of handing out incentive checks to my staff!

4. Set up Special Incentive Plans.

❑ I often took advantage of the holiday season to help my staff with their holiday shopping. I would put together fun games, such as giving stylists play money if they surpassed their specific goal. This play money was banked away for that stylist to "spend" on education, hair shows, or tools. It was a great way to encourage stylists to build a nest egg for special events. It taught them how to budget their money as well, which is something I found to be necessary in this profession.

❑ Any time stylists doubled their sales over the prior week, they received a $10 gift card to a local coffee shop. Even a little praise can go a long way.

❑ This next program was very successful at fostering healthy competition between my stylists:
   • Three times a year, I would split my staff into teams. The team that sold the most products in a specified month would get a steak dinner. The team that lost got pizza. I always wanted to promote the feeling of winning for everyone.

5. Track Sales.

Tracking sales is very important and should be set up in a highly visible area in the back room for all your staff to view. Use any kind of chart such as a thermometer, map, dartboard, race (such as a steeple chase, see **Figure 1** below), or any other visual aid that has start and end points and moveable pieces so that the chart can be used to follow each stylist's success.

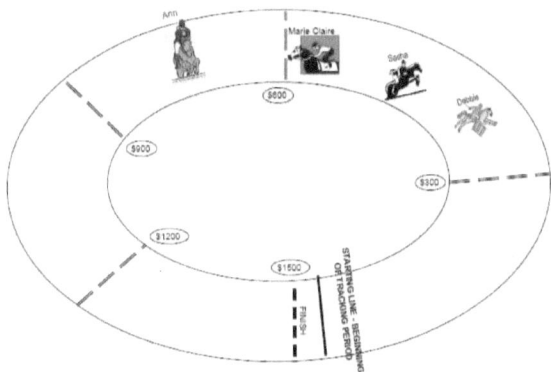

Figure 1. Example of a steeple chase chart.

Track your staff's sales by the week or month and celebrate each success!

Remember, the keys to keeping your staff focused on retailing in your salon are:

1. Constant and continued focus.
2. Fair and equitable base incentive plans for stylists and managers.
3. Special incentive plans for stretch goals.
4. Setting and measuring weekly and monthly targets.
5. Celebrate each and every success, no matter how big or small.
6. Praise goes a long, long way.

I also used vacation vouchers as retailing incentives very successfully with my stylists.

These certificates are not connected in any way with time share opportunities, and they are so inexpensive for owners to purchase! I had terrific success utilizing these vacation vouchers as stylist incentives. For example, I would give a certificate to stylists who sold over $x amount of retail during a month or special promotion. You can also give them to your stylists as a holiday gift. I saw a significant increase in sales because my team was motivated to out-perform. I also found the certificates were a perk that enabled me to more easily retain my top performers. Because I believe so strongly in these certificates, I offer them directly on my website. For more information and to learn how to purchase these incentive certificates, go to www. PositiveSalonStrategies.com and click on "Vacation Certificates."

Which of the retailing incentive programs you have just read would you like to try first?

_____

_____

_____

What other retailing incentive programs will you create?

_____

_____

_____

_____

_____

Although products don't sell themselves, as I mentioned earlier, an attractive display of your products is important. Salon owners should step back and look at their retail shelves with the eyes of a client. Don't hesitate to move things around the salon to create an ideal setup in all the areas of your salon. Your retail shelves should be very inviting so that the client will want to look through the products.

Many stores often change their displays on a regular basis. I used this method in my salons. If you don't change things up, the client will soon become oblivious to her surroundings when entering your salon.

Let your windows also do advertising for your salon.

Dress up the window with product sales, product of the month, and displays to go with the season or the holi- day. Hanukkah, Christmas, Valentine's Day, Easter, Thanksgiving are among the many opportunities you have to dress up your windows.

Let the window tell a story. A customer will immediately know that you are also a retail salon.

Support your staffs' retailing efforts by getting the word out to your customers, too. Many companies can assist with tools such as posters, shelf talkers, and displays of the products you have purchased from them. Make sure you utilize these materials. Usually they are complimentary! Place new products on styling stations to kick-start conversations between your stylist and customer. Use the stylists' stations for product specials and any other ideas that will help the stylist to remember to talk product.

Don't forget the 100% satisfaction guarantee. Satisfied customers are the foundation of any business. This policy really helped my staff to feel more comfortable about selling new product to clients because they knew the client could always bring it back for an in-store cred- it or an exchange for another product. All products should be guaranteed, and you only want the very best products for your business. My salon guaranteed everything we sold because we firmly believed in the products that we carried.

Look around your salon. What are the best locations for promotional materials, displays and products to be placed?

_____

_____

_____

So let's look at some other ways to have fun and help your stylists to stay focused on selling retail. The added bonus is that these tips are designed to be financially rewarding as well.

❑   Try to create promotional packages for various products each month. I used to create a theme for each promotion, usually centering the theme around the season, holidays and special occasions.

JANUARY is a great month to START THE NEW YEAR WITH A NEW YOU.

This advertises to clients that change is always available for their hair, skin, and nails. This month can be a slow-down month for retail since it comes right after the holidays. There- fore, it is an especially good time to create incentive retail programs for your stylists and incentive purchasing programs for your clients. For example, you could offer a facial and total makeup make-over and offer $25.00 worth of product free. If your salon is in a cold area, you can offer a free take-home moisturizing conditioner with each color service.

FEBRUARY was my favorite time of year to put promotional packages together. I would make packages for both men and women with Valentine's Day in mind. I would make packages with men's products for the wife to buy, and vice versa. I made little baskets with kids shampoo, conditioner and gels, and I would put candy hearts all over the basket. These were always a huge winner.

MARCH & APRIL bring spring, and Easter was

such a fun time to create packages for kids and parents. I would design kid's packages with chocolate eggs, jelly beans and some of our favorite children's hair products such as color gels.

I would have the staff show these to our mothers and fathers to entice them to buy.

I also made adult baskets with candy and plastic eggs that contained a surprise percentage off their next visit.

I would shrink wrap moisturizing shampoo and conditioner, and I would make baskets with makeup for mom and baskets of men's gel and body wash for dad.

In MAY, Mother's Day has always been a traditional celebration of appreciation for the best mothers in the world. Gift certificates and a variety of shrink-wrapped retail products were always winners.

JUNE is Father's Day, and we would do the same.

In the SUMMER time, I would decorate my salon with a summer, beach theme. I would put products together with beach towels and leave-in conditioners to protect the hair from the sun. I would also put together clarifying shampoo and treatments for the swimmer to cleanse salts or chlorine out of the hair.

In addition, I would put packages together geared for the skin to protect it from the sun.

AUGUST was the perfect time to promote back to school hairstyles that are gorgeous and easy to maintain.

I filled little plastic lunch boxes with children's products for back to school.

For junior high, high school, and college-aged clients, I would create a package of age-appropriate make up and skin care to add a natural fresh look.

In August, we also did very well with liter sales, usually by offering 2 liters for $20.00 that we normally sold for $35.00. They flew off the shelf.

FALL was a great time to promote rejuvenation for tired, dull hair. Often times, chlorine, sun, and salt water will really damage the hair and skin when not protected carefully. I offered in-salon deep protein conditioner treatments along with a hydrat- ing moisture mask.

Fall is also a great time for salons to run a color service promotion, cross merchandising with home maintenance products. This will encourage the client to purchase professional products that will keep the hair in a healthy state. For example, with every color service you get 25% off any product of your choice.

In NOVEMBER it is time to get ready for the holidays and to create holiday package promotions.

Gift certificates, stocking stuffers, and gift baskets should be the center of attention in your salon. You can also cross promote up-do services with manicures, pedicures, and facials. A one-stop shop is very popular, where the client can get several services at a great promotional price.

❏ Another tool that is great for any time of year is the wonderful incentive program I mentioned earlier in this workshop which utilizes vacation certificates as an incentive to encourage clients to spend more in your salon. It is a value added strategy that is a complete winner. When I discussed them earlier, I mentioned I used these certificates as performance incentives for my staff.

The certificates are great for clients too. You can give your clients vacation certificates as a reward for purchasing services and products at your salon. Your existing clients will have an incentive to return more frequently and spend more money. You will attract new clients and generate referrals, too, because who wouldn't want a free 3 day/2 night hotel stay! Please visit my website at www.PositiveSalonStrategies.com to learn more about vacation vouchers.

Again, the ideas are endless. Be creative and have fun!

In summary, there are seven simple rules of retailing for salon professionals to remember that will help them begin to retail successfully. Teach your stylists the following:

1. Remember you are <u>serving</u> the client NOT selling to her.
2. Find common interests with your client during the consultation. This will send the message that you find this person interesting enough to engage in conversation, and it will create a bond be- tween you.
3. Listen to the tone, tempo, and speed in which your client is speaking and try and match it.
4. If a client says she does not want to buy a product, it most often means

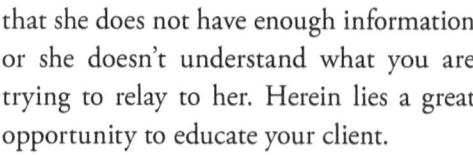

that she does not have enough information or she doesn't understand what you are trying to relay to her. Herein lies a great opportunity to educate your client.

5.   Take all the information that you receive from your client during the consultation and use

this knowledge to suggest a variety of services that may interest her.

6. Keep in mind that making powerful recommendations will increase your service and retail sales.
7. Remember something that good wait staff know: They are likely to receive higher tips

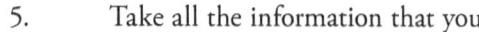

when they make knowledgeable suggestions to their customers about food and drinks that are on the menu.

It shows they know their business.

I have taught these rules of retailing for years and have used them with the staff in my own salons as well.

I know that all the proven tips we have covered in this book work, and I also know that you will be successful when you implement them into your clients' consultations and during the time you are servicing your clients too.

Remember that retailing should be a part of each salon service. Putting a solid plan in action to increase your retail sales should be a crucial component of your business plan. Retail sales can account for incredibly increased profits. You want your retail sales to pay your bills and that should be one of your business goals.

I hope you have enjoyed this workbook, Retailing in Action, and I wish you all the success for your salon!

Retailing in Action Worksheet

Do you carry products that motivate and excite your staff?
Yes_____   No_____

Do you offer product training to all members of your staff?
Yes_____   No_____

Do your stylists use your salon's products?
Yes_____   No_____   Some_____

Do you send products home regularly with your stylists so they can become personally familiar with all the products' benefits and features?
Yes_____   No_____

Do you talk with your stylists about what products they like and what products they don't like?

Yes_____   No_____

Do you involve your entire team when deciding what products to carry?

Yes_____   No_____

Do you work with companies that provide product education training for your staff?

Yes_____   No_____

What stylist retailing incentives do you use?

_____

_____

_____

_____

_____

Are your products displayed neatly and attractively?

Yes_____   No_____   Somewhat_____

Do you change your displays regularly?

Yes_____   No_____   Not as often as I should_____

Do you dress up your windows and change the displays with the seasons and/or holidays?

Yes_____   No_____

Do you utilize complimentary tools and materials from your product companies?

Yes_____   No_____

What type of product satisfaction guarantee do you, or will you, provide for your customers?

_____

_____

_____

My action plan for creating promotional packages to help my stylists stay focused on selling retail and to increase my retail sales will be:

_____

_____

_____

_____

_____

_____

_____

_____

Additional Thoughts:

_____

_____

_____

_____

_____

_____

_____

Sample of texture menus:

TEXTURE DESIGN MENU

Making Waves
Luxurious alternating wave pat- terns that move in the direction that best suits your hair.

Bodifying or Volumizing Treatmentw
Amplify the fullness and thick- ness of your hair texture with- out adding curl.

Style Support
Texture to create life and volume at the base of the hair shaft to support the finished design.

Structurizing
Define your hair style by adding silky, voluminous texture. By alternating the size and direction of curl, you enhance shape and add dimension to your style.

The Design Direction
As individual as you are, this texture technique follows the design lines of your desired hair style to create a low maintenance, easy-care yet fashionable finish.

Spiral Texture Service

From loose spiraled formations to coiled ringlets of curl, the results are soft, feminine and creative.

Zonal or Partial Waves

A technique of adding partial support or hidden movement only in the design areas that require added texture treatment.

Texture a la Carte

Texture – where you need it or want it. Add a few waves in those problem areas for style, support, or personalized effects.

Sample of Texture Menus:

TEXTURE TREATMENT MENU

Curl Reducer Treatment

Change the wave pattern of natural curls or relax too tight or curly hair.

Curl Straightener Treatment

Remove all natural waves and curls for shiny and silky straight hair styles. Treat perm regrowth and straighten to natural state as hair is growing out.

Hair Softening Treatment

Re-texture coarse, wiry hair to a soft and manageable texture.

Directional Texture

Redesign hair growth patterns by taking con- trol of cowlicks and neck line patterns or change wave patterns in specific areas, like the fringe.

ABOUT THE AUTHOR

Jeanne Degen is a leader in the beauty industry. For 33 years, she has brought her expertise to salons, manufacturers and distributorships as an educator, a trainer, a stylist and as a successful salon owner. Now she has created Positive Salon Strategies, a salon consulting company that delivers easily accessible, proven business strategies to salon professionals in the beauty profession.

Her 10-minute online workshops are designed as easy to follow, step-by-step instructional programs that allow salon professionals to learn effective techniques for business success. The workshops feature tips and strategies that Jeanne herself used to manage and grow her salon business. She knows how hectic running a salon can be, and she is confident and excited that the short format instruction provided by Positive Salon Strategies will help others to be more successful at operating their businesses.

Jeanne brings impressive professional experience to bear in her company. As Director of Operations and Education at Fantastic Sam's International Corp, she has assisted franchisees nationwide to build salon revenue. She not only offered education and operational support to established salons, but also supervised and conducted new salon opening trainings, including interviewing and hiring new staff. She has taught and created workshops that address employee turnover, that motivate staff to sell, create winning salon promotions, power retailing, and that help create great customer service, among many other topics. Jeanne also consulted with salon owners and franchisees on profitability, inventory control, client retention, and all business aspects necessary for operating a successful salon.

Jeanne has also held positions at internationally acclaimed companies, including Brand Manager at Artec in support of Goldwell Distributors, National Director of Education at ISO and National Education and Sales Manager at Helene Curtis. She has hands-on stylist experience and has performed platform work with some of the most elite platform artists in the industry. Most importantly, Jeanne is thrilled to realize her dream of supporting the growth and prosperity of the salon community through her company, Positive Salon Strategies.